FREE OFFER

Ever wonder what damage a hacker can do after you click a phishing email link?

We have the answer!

We will run our phishing simulator on your company computers so you can learn what your vulnerabilities are and what steps you can take to better protect your company. How it works:

1. We sign a nondisclosure agreement because we will uncover sensitive information.
2. We schedule a meeting so I can ask some questions before we start.
3. We email you a link to share with three people in your company.
4. You share the link and make sure everyone clicks it.
5. We schedule a time to go over the results via a Zoom.

I will not need administrative credentials. And I will not install anything on your computer. **You must have at least ten company computers to participate!**

Sign up here: https://NextCenturyTech.com/phish

Or scan here:

Also by Tracy Hardin:

How to Manage IT in Your Business:
A Guide to Demystifying IT Operations for
Small and Medium Businesses

What You Need to Know About IT
Without the Geek-Speak

HOW TO
CYBER SECURE
YOUR BUSINESS

A Guide to Demystifying IT Security
for Small and Medium Businesses

TRACY HARDIN

DISCLAIMER:

While all attempts have been made to verify information provided in this publication, neither the author nor the publisher assumes any responsibility for errors, omissions or contradictory interpretation of the subject matter herein. This publication is designed to provide accurate and authoritative information with regards to the subject matter covered. However, it is sold with the understanding that the author and the publisher are not engaged in rendering legal, accounting, or other professional advice. If professional advice or other expert assistance is required, the services of a competent professional should be sought. The purchaser or reader of this publication assumes responsibility for the use of these materials and information. Adherence to all applicable laws and regulations, including federal, state and local governing professional licensing, business practices, advertising and any other aspects of doing business is the sole responsibility of the purchaser or reader.

CONTENTS

Part 5—Glossary

I dedicate this book to my parents.
They never held me back.
They let me live my dream, and I am eternally
grateful for their support.
I so miss them.

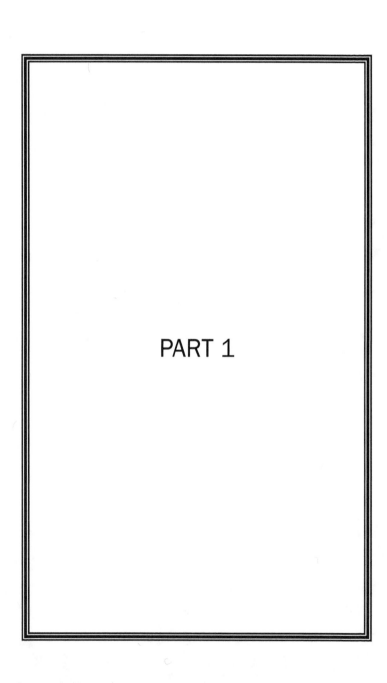

PART 1

WELCOME

FOREWORD

The rapid advancement of technology in recent years has never failed to fascinate me. Three decades ago, the concept of a hard drive being held for ransom would have been laughable. Who are we, a spy whose identity is being threatened by Dr. Evil? Yet, today, it is an occurrence so commonplace that new reports of outages or breaches scarcely cause surprise. Yet, many small business owners remain rooted in an outdated mindset, telling themselves, "It won't happen to me."

This book provides an engaging introduction to the landscape of cyber threats and data breaches, with a focus on the vulnerabilities that small businesses face. Instead of resorting to fearmongering, it emphasizes the importance of understanding these risks to your company so you can properly treat them.

I draw from nearly 20 years of experience in information technology (IT), largely focusing on information security and digital forensics. I have earned a master's degree in cyber forensics and security, countless certifications, and serve as a Sr. Digital Forensic Investigator at one of the nation's top law firms. Time and time again, I have seen small businesses suffer losses that could have been prevented by applying the principles in this book. Despite rapid technological evolution, the fundamentals of information security tend to remain quite stable.

I first connected with Tracy through several IT forums. We always seemed to comment on similar threads due to our passion for the security industry and for helping people. Since then, we have met in person at a number of conferences and presented in security presentations together. I have even had the pleasure of working with her company on a few occasions. It has always struck me how well Tracy can break down complex technical topics so that anyone can understand while she simultaneously conveys the technical details and verbosity required for these complex topics. You'll certainly appreciate Tracy's clarity throughout the book.

While technical safeguards and specialized services play crucial roles in cyber defense, keeping your business safe starts with you. Learning about the threats your business faces and how they work enables you to be the first line of defense. This is important—it doesn't matter how well the technical controls work; security is ultimately in the hands of the people who run the business. It also enables you to understand the benefit (or lack thereof) of any controls or policies your business currently utilizes.

In addition to learning about the various types of threats your business can face, this book gives you practical tips on how to combat those threats. Whether you work with an internal IT team, outsourced IT provider, manage your own IT equipment, or operate a local spy agency looking to protect your agents from Dr. Evil, this book is for you. At the end of the book, you will find a practical checklist to help gauge the cyber-maturity level of your small business.

–Brian Semrau
Sr. Digital Forensic Investigator/Director of IT,
Edelson PC
Adjunct Professor of Computer Information Systems,
Triton College
Founder, Infosec Chicago

Please note:

Italicized words and phrases are found
in the Glossary!

WHO SHOULD READ
THIS BOOK?

This book is written for those who are responsible for IT at their company. Depending on the size of the organization, this can be the CEO, COO, office manager or VP, sometimes the CFO. These folks may have an IT Pro they can call, or they may have to fill that role along with their other duties.

Hackers are a threat to any company with computers, and it's critical that business leaders take this threat seriously. So why am I writing a book? I'm a consultant; helping people is what I love to do. Being educated about these threats is the first step to stopping these threats.

I get a lot more questions about cybersecurity than ever before, and I understand the concern. Often, I see the person saddled with overseeing IT doesn't have the time, skillset, or desire to tackle this never-ending project. It's no easy feat—there are hacking pros out there daily trying their best to steal money from you through your computers.

In this book, I often mention compliance regulations for medical and financial industries, but ANY industry is a target today. Hackers know that companies that don't fall under regulatory compliance tend to spend less on cybersecurity, so their defenses are not as good. Automated attacks that are run by *bots* make it easy to send a *phishing email* to 100,000 people for very little time and money. All it takes is for just a few people to click and it's a success.

MY PROMISE TO YOU

I promise this book will help you have a better understanding of the risks posed by cybersecurity threats without all the geek-speak. In the book, I will refer to your "IT Pro." This is someone that is your IT go-to for support, buying advice, and general IT consultation. This person may be on your staff, or may work for an IT company like mine, or a trusted individual that you can pick up the phone and call. This person should have in-depth knowledge of your IT environment.

After reading this book, you should sit down with your IT Pro and go over my cybersecurity checklist to see where you can make improvements. You will feel more confident when you do spend the money securing your IT. Now is the time to get that cyber insurance policy because you know what to expect on the application and can answer the questions correctly.

I don't shy away from all the technical terms because they are everywhere in the headlines of online articles and videos, and you need to know them. So, if you see a technical term *italicized*, you know you can find out more about it in the Glossary of this book.

I recommend reading the entire Glossary because news articles and videos will have much more meaning.

INTRODUCTION

My name is Tracy Hardin. I am the president and founder of Next Century Technologies, an IT consulting firm located in Lexington, KY. I was introduced to computers in the early 1980's when my parents bought me my first computer, a Commodore VIC-20, for Christmas. I was interested in computers, so I took all the computer math courses that my high school offered. Since I found my computer classes to be easy, I picked computer science to be my college major. Luckily for me, it turned out to be a good choice!

In the late 80's, the University of Kentucky had several large computer mainframes which were used for research and for all my computer science courses. However, I really enjoyed working in the University's computer labs as a consultant to help the students and faculty. There I got introduced to Novell NetWare, the most popular operating system at the time for personal computer networks. To earn my bachelor's degree, I did a lot of programming classes and quickly learned that was not for me. Managing personal computer networks with Novell was much more engaging.

I graduated from the University of Kentucky with a computer science degree in 1990. My years of experience as a student consultant at the University's various labs really helped because the nation was in a recession and jobs were scarce. I spent the next ten years working in the corporate world. I worked for two government contractors, a third-party benefits management company, a large bank-holding company and finally with a small computer consulting firm here in Lexington. Along the way, I got my Novell NetWare certification so I could build and design computer networks, which became the focus of my IT career.

Working for a computer consulting firm sparked a new love for me—helping businesses in all kinds of industries with IT. I really enjoyed seeing what goes on behind the scenes at these companies and how they leverage IT to improve their bottom line. I also learned a lot about how to not run a company while working for that consulting firm and considered just going out on my own. Luckily, I was fired from that job right before Thanksgiving in 2000 for volunteering my IT skills at my church. While I didn't miss my old boss, I did miss the clients I was serving. I sent out Christmas cards to them with holiday wishes and that I would miss them. Soon, they all tracked me down via the return address on the envelope. These former clients became the foundation of what would become my foray into self-employment.

My new company, Woodford Computer Solutions (named for the Kentucky county I lived in at the time), was started on January 1, 2001. I had a home office, a laptop, a bag of tools and a pickup truck. My focus would be helping businesses with their computers. Back then, IT was a small enough world for me to be very effective at managing computer networks in all types of sectors, including insurance, TV/radio, construction, banking, medical and various professional services.

A few years later, I moved to Lexington and changed the company name to Next Century Technologies, in honor of the new century we were in. My company grew by word-of-mouth; I did no advertising. By 2012, I had dozens of small business clients. The threat landscape had changed dramatically with *malware* rendering workstations and servers completely unusable. My business model became a "Managed Services Provider" (MSP) instead of the old you-break-it-and-I-fix-it model. I didn't simply install antivirus and walk away; I installed antivirus and a management agent on every workstation and began proactively monitoring stuff. I didn't see a choice. Viruses and *malware* were becoming too sophisticated, and computers were being infected from just browsing the wrong website. I had to be more involved and needed better technical tools to properly protect my clients. In 2012, I had to hire my first employees to help with the workload as word-of-mouth referrals quickly outpaced my ability to keep up.

It's 2024, and I am seeing more client emails successfully hacked than ever before. I have a team of 8 folks in my office to help me manage and support close to 700 computers plus dozens of projects. We've had an uptick in companies with their own IT departments reaching out to us to help their teams manage IT. I wish I could write that the technology defenses have kept up with the hackers, but sadly, they have not. Educating yourself and hiring the right IT experts is the best defense...for now!

—Tracy Hardin

FREE OFFER TO READERS

Sign up for our tech tips!

Each tip takes less than 30 seconds to read but gives you critical info on avoiding online scams, ransom attacks, or other mistakes that can cost you.

Sign up here:

https://NextCenturyTech.com/techtips

Or scan here:

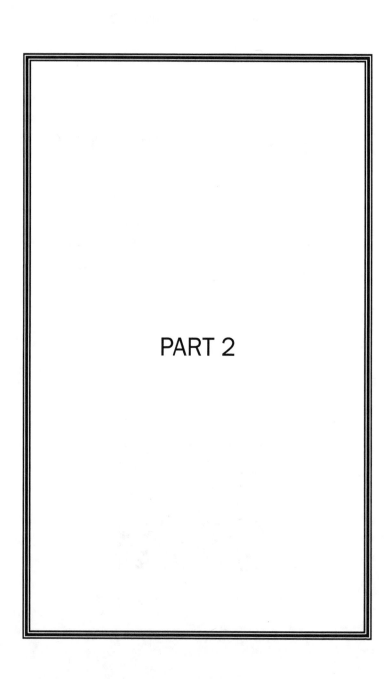

PART 2

IDENTIFYING THE
CYBER THREATS

CHAPTER 1

VIRUSES AND MALWARE

I got my first introduction to *viruses* as a student consultant in the computer lab at the University of Kentucky. The Macintosh computers were notorious for spreading viruses via the autoloading features of the floppy disk drives.

IBM was also a big University sponsor and had provided the lab with over a dozen new IBM desktops, but the Macs were most popular with the students, and unfortunately, the most unsecure. Ironically, many folks claim that Macs are more secure. Well, that wasn't always the case, and nowadays, no operating system is immune from viruses, *worms*, or other malware. When Al Gore "invented" the internet in the 90's (urban legend but still funny), the government pumped yet more money into improving the size, quality, and speed of the internet. Businesses made websites, and every employee got an email. New threats evolved, and simple antivirus was no longer enough.

A virus, by definition, replicates itself. It finds a host operating system (think Windows or Mac) and inserts its own code into operating system files. It can also insert itself into a host program, like Word or Excel. They can also be found in spreadsheet macros. Computer worms, on the other hand, do not need a host program. They are stand-alone programs and do not rely on a host. Identifying compromised host files or questionable new programs is part of what antivirus software does.

Advertising-supported software or adware is software developed to generate income through advertising. There was a time when pop-ups on websites were everywhere trying to get you to buy a product or service. Spyware was often imbedded in adware to collect and report on what the user was clicking on. It became so bad that the adware and spyware would install itself on your computer, making for a miserable experience of endless pop-ups even if you were not connected to the internet. Antivirus quickly expanded to include anti-adware and anti-spyware. The term malware was coined to cover all these threats, including viruses and worms.

Once, I got a call from a small marketing firm who had a computer that was down. I found the computer to be so infected with malware that the screen-covered pop-ups rendered the system unusable. Their antivirus subscription had run out, and they had not renewed it. I had no choice but to wipe out the computer and start over. Three hours later, the computer was back online, but the user's afternoon was pretty much over. The "free" antivirus the marketing firm was using had cost them dearly.

I often hear people say about malware creators, "Don't these people have anything better to do with their time?" Well, there are a variety of motives behind these types of attacks. Those include making money, making a political statement, boredom, amusement, to prove a point on a software *vulnerability*, or for bragging rights.

Today Microsoft has included a pretty good anti-malware program within the Windows operating system called Microsoft Defender. However, I have never recommended Defender alone for a business computer. The next-gen antivirus includes *endpoint detection and response* or *EDR* functions. EDR allows your antivirus to do more. It can provide additional protection against *ransomware* and offer forensic information if a breach does occur. EDR also utilizes *artificial intelligence* (*AI*) to help identify threats by looking for suspicious activities. XDR or extended detection and response goes a step further by looking at traffic from the *cloud*, email, and other endpoints, such as computers and servers. *MDR* is *managed detection and response*. With MDR, there is a team that acts on alerts for you, 24 hours a day. MDR offers the best protection unless you have your own staff ready to act on an alert at 3AM.

CHAPTER 2

RANSOMWARE

Did you know the first case of ransomware goes back to 1989? It really grew quickly in 2013 thanks to *cryptocurrency* offering an "untraceable" method of payment (note the quotes there; it's not really untraceable).

I've grown weary of seeing US-based companies getting attacked by foreign hackers who can't be arrested. In many cases, hackers are well-financed, well-organized, and well-staffed in office buildings that function as legitimate businesses in their home countries. There is really nothing the US government can do to stop the onslaught, nothing our military can do to defend us business owners on this virtual battlefield.

Ransomware is a type of malware that encrypts or locks files and demands payment to get them released. Ransomware became more popular with the advent of cryptocurrency. Even with the deep pockets of big corporations and more sophisticated technical defenses, ransomware pays well. It's not going away anytime soon.

Why Should Business Owners Be Worried About Ransomware?

Ransomware is more than just encrypting files. Not only is the data encrypted, but the data is also copied, and the hackers request payment from the victim to prevent that data from being publicly displayed. Hackers will also use the data, which often includes *personally identifiable information* (*PII*), to build a list of new victims to attack.

Ransomware and data extortion has been making headline news lately and interrupting millions of American lives. Just last week, the UnitedHealth Group allegedly paid a $22M ransom to recover the data for their subsidiary, Change Healthcare. The city of Dallas, TX, came under attack in May of 2023 and shut down many city services and exposed personal data for over 30,000 citizens. The Las Vegas MGM Resorts® attack in September of that same year made headlines when a massive leak of personal customer data occurred. Many hotels and casinos suffered disruptions and shutdowns. MGM estimated losses at $100M. Finally, we all remember the Colonial Pipeline shutdown in May of 2021, which affected far more than the Southeast, when Americans all across the country panicked and rushed to fill their gas tanks, causing gas shortages in areas not even served by Colonial. That attack highlighted just how vulnerable we all are to ransomware attacks when our critical infrastructure is so dependent upon technology.

Ransomware has been around for a long time with the past few years seeing an exponential growth both in the number of attacks and in the ransom amounts. The year 2023 saw double the number of attacks seen in 2022 according to Corvus Insurance. The hackers have fine-tuned ransomware into a successful business model, complete with brick-and-mortar office buildings, staff, human resources, everything you would find in any successful business endeavor. All of this is overseas, of course, where they are out of reach, for the most part, from US authorities.

Around 2021, the BlackCat/ALPHV ransomware group was created to offer "ransomware-as-a-service." Freelance hackers can earn a commission by partnering with the BlackCat group to ransom the data found on the networks they hack. They are known as the first group to provide a website for public data leaks. They would post excerpts of the data to prove it was genuine, which is important when threatening to release victims' data. They are behind the ransomware attacks on both MGM and Change Health, plus many more, possibly hundreds of others. Groups like BlackCat incentivize hackers to attack more and more targets—companies like yours.

How Does Ransomware Get In?

GalacticAdvisors.com reports that, in 2023, the number one method of attack was done by malicious emails. Next was stealing login credentials, and the third popular method was exploiting existing vulnerabilities in hardware and software. Let's look at each method briefly.

Malicious Emails

Phishing emails try to get victims to click links that allow malicious software to load. This same software could try to grab unsecure login credentials on your computer or install a backdoor in your system for later use, such as installing ransomware or copying critical data. Phishing emails may also include links that try to get you to enter your email password or the credentials for your credit card login so they can be stolen.

Login Credentials

Login credentials include not only your password to log into your computer in the morning but also the ones for your email, *cloud* applications, and websites.

How do login credentials get stolen anyway? A fake website could fool you into entering your email password. Reusing a password across multiple websites means that a hacker that steals data from just one website will have your password to try on other websites or emails. Another example would be storing your passwords in a Word or Excel file or within a web browser, like Chrome, allowing hackers easy access if they get into your computer. A final example would be using easily guessable passwords.

Brute force attacks use trial and error to "guess" a password. With today's computers, an automated brute force attack can make hundreds of guesses a second. A random eight-character password with all lowercase letters can be hacked almost immediately. There are several types of brute force attacks, but a popular method is to start with a list of well-known passwords, which are easily found online. Microsoft recommends passwords that are at least 12 characters long and have a mixture of uppercase and lowercase letters, numbers, and symbols. A password manager can help with keeping long unique passwords for all your sites and software.

Exploited Vulnerabilities

Vulnerabilities are weaknesses in software application security. An application relies on a lot of different layers of programming to function properly. The operating system it runs on has a massive amount of code. The network devices that transfer the data from one computer to another also run on yet more code. Much software code is reused, which is good in terms of efficiency, but any weaknesses in that code will appear in multiple applications and even devices. A rush to market a new software or device may result in a lack of focus by the programmer on security. Hackers know this and spend a lot of time testing applications, operating systems, and network devices to see what weaknesses they can manipulate. When these weaknesses are discovered, hackers will share them with others.

A recent example of an exploited vulnerability attack was the MOVEit compromise. MOVEit is a file transfer app whose compromise affected tens of millions of people. With one hack, a massive breach occurred across THOUSANDS of companies, including Indiana Medicaid, British Airways, US Dept of Energy, various pension funds, nonprofits, financial firms, and many more government organizations. A *zero-day vulnerability* allowed hackers to gain access to data that was ransomed. The hackers added their malware to the MOVEit application so they could steal data. They also threatened to reveal the data on their websites if payment was not made.

Three Common Myths About Ransomware

1. **My company is too small to be a target.** Do you have money? If so, then you are a target. As an IT consultant, I've seen the damage hackers can do to businesses that are too "small." Most ransomware attacks go unreported, and the small company attacks are not sensational enough to make the headlines. Don't be fooled—it's a big threat to the business owners' livelihoods when their IT assets are under attack.

2. **I have cybersecurity insurance, so I have nothing to worry about.** Nothing is further from the truth. Cybersecurity insurance does not guarantee you will receive the key to unlock your data or that stolen data will be deleted. Hackers download your data and go through it to see if they can extort money from YOUR clients as well. This is disastrous to any company's reputation. Also, most cyber policies now require certain security standards to be met on the network in order for a claim to not be denied. In other words, you cannot turn a blind eye to cybersecurity and expect your policy to cover everything.

3. **My IT person/company has me covered.** No, they don't. No one has a 100% effective defense against hackers. If you have hired an IT firm to manage your IT, look closely at your support contract. You will likely see verbiage excluding the hours spent recovering from an attack, and nowhere does it guarantee one will not happen.

Summary

Ransomware is still making big headlines due to the impact it has on big corporations. For companies that still rely on their own file servers, it's a huge threat. So, if you rely on your own servers, be sure to check out Part 3 of this book that focuses on the prevention of attacks.

Companies that store data in the cloud are less threatened by ransomware. However, ransomcloud is growing in popularity, and several types focus on encrypting files in OneDrive. Big payouts and lack of security means ransomware is not going away anytime soon.

CHAPTER 3

THE GREATEST VULNERABILITY OF THEM ALL

E mail is such a critical tool in the scope of business operations that it's hard to imagine any
company doing business without it. Yet email offers a
hacker a window of access to your employees. In this
chapter, I will focus on security for Microsoft 365,
arguably the most popular business email platform in
the US. However, the *security vulnerabilities* of the
365 platform are common across all email platforms,
so don't feel like you should skip this chapter just
because you have a Google mailbox.

At the time of this writing, the year 2024 has just
begun. My company rolled out a new Microsoft 365
email monitoring tool the last quarter of 2023, and
we have already identified and stopped four email
compromises on three clients in just the first four
weeks. What are hackers gaining from this? Why did

our clients not realize their emails were compromised? Your data is valuable, and with your email password, hackers get all this and more:

- Copies of all your emails, including content that could include financial information.
- Your contact list along with the associated *PII*.
- Your employee list.
- Access to your inbox rules.
- A copy of your email signature.

With a copy of your emails, email signature, and contact list, hackers can now impersonate you to your own co-workers, customers, vendors, and friends. Hackers will send emails with malicious links embedded from your mailbox to all your contacts. Since it's a legitimate email from a trusted person, your contacts are very likely to click that malicious link.

A perfect example of this is when the office manager of one of our larger clients had her email quietly compromised. The hackers noticed that she moved a large amount of money every two weeks for payroll via the local community bank. The hackers, pretending to be the office manager, emailed the bank requesting that the payroll be redirected to a new account overseas. This bank was not one of our clients, but we do have bank clients, so I know the employee had extensive cybersecurity training as required for financial compliance. However, she sent the hacker back the form to fill out to make this change. The hacker returned the form, and the poor English prompted the banker to call the office manager.

Thankfully, payroll for over 150 employees was not sent overseas, but you can see how profitable and easy this scam is to pull off by just stealing email credentials. In this case, I was able to narrow down how the email credentials were likely compromised. She was a long-time client and was very diligent about not clicking any link. (I had installed a good amount of skepticism in her!) However, she was using an online HR program, and that was the only site that shared the same username and password as her email. It was never proven, but it's my theory that this HR site was breached, and the username and password list was stolen by a hacker, possibly sold on the *dark web*. *Two-factor authentication* (*2FA*) on the office manager's mailbox would have stopped the hacker. Fortunately, events like these motivate companies to enable 2FA.

In the story above, hackers deleted sent emails and rerouted new ones via mailbox rules so they could easily hide their tracks from the office manager. This is a very popular and successful method for hackers to profit off their victims. So how do the hackers get the passwords?

Here are some of the ways they could get them:

- The victim clicks on a link in a phishing email. That link looks like it is from Microsoft and asks the victim to confirm their username and password.

- The victim recycles the same password across multiple sites, and one of those sites gets breached.

- The password is easy to guess, so a brute force attack is used successfully.

- The password is on the dark web, and the victim doesn't know it.

- The victim clicks on a malicious link in an email that is compromised, and the link captures their Microsoft username, password and *2FA* code (sign-in token hijacking).

- *Social engineering* leads the victim or help desk to provide the username and password to a hacker over the phone.

- Hardware devices on the network with security vulnerabilities allows hackers to get into the network and steal unprotected passwords.

- *Legacy authentication* is in use by the email provider, which offers less protection.

A lot of damage can be done via email without having credentials compromised. One very popular scam happened to one of our clients, a construction contractor. Jim had been working with an out-of-state property developer on a hotel project here in Lexington. Jim never received payment from the developer. He reached out and the developer sent proof, via email, that Jim had requested the payment be redirected to a different bank account. In a panic, Jim called me because he didn't remember sending that email. I told Jim to forward the email to me. At first glance, the email looked legit, even had Jim's custom email signature with company logo. But I quickly realized the "FROM" address was off. The email's domain name (the part after the @ symbol) for Jim's company had two letters switched. It was a long domain name and easy to miss. This hacker had gone to the trouble of purchasing the domain name purposely misspelling it.

Why did the hacker target Jim's company? Likely the email address for the developer was compromised at some point, so they knew the property developer did business with Jim's company. They also got the names and email signatures of everyone involved in the hotel project. Having that information made it worth the effort to buy a domain name slightly different than Jim's. How much money did the property developer send to the hackers? Around

$380K. This is a great example of why small businesses make such great targets for hackers—they can and will make big financial transactions and often do not spend a lot of money on cybersecurity. Both my client and the developer involved were small businesses. So, did the developers lose all their money? No. They did open a case with the FBI, and last I heard, they had gotten most, but not all, of it back. They were lucky to get anything back.

A couple of days after Jim's scare with the email scammers, I gave Jim a call and asked if he had a cyber insurance policy. He said he did. I then asked him what would've happened if the hackers really did steal his email credentials? Would his company have to pay back the $380,000? He said, "Let me talk to my agent." He called me back later that day and said, "No, my policy would not have covered that loss. But I updated my policy, and it does now." Would your insurance policy pay if your email credentials were involved in a theft? Doesn't hurt to ask.

What Can One Click Do?

A whole bunch! That's why phishing emails can cause so much damage so quickly. One of my favorite tools is a phishing simulator that I run on my clients' computers or on prospects' computers. I email one link to the target user and ask them to click it. With one click, I can get in a single report:

- A list of passwords stored on that computer. I always find passwords.
- Detailed information on the devices found on the company network, such as *firewalls*, workstations, and servers.
- Customer *PII*, including credit card numbers, social security numbers, names, addresses, and phone numbers from files stored on that computer.
- Employee PII, especially on human resources and executive computers. This can include direct-deposit information and health insurance information.
- Which computers have unencrypted hard drives.
- Vulnerabilities found across the network and accessible from the internet.
- The type of antivirus installed.
- Remote access software installed on computers.
- The domain name for the local server.
- Their operating system version.
- Missing patches for operating systems.
- A list of applications installed on the computer.
- Their hard-drive size and space available.

- Shared drives out on the company network, including access to all the data on those other computers.
- Open ports on the computer and local firewall.
- *Microsoft 365 sign-in tokens* found (which means email compromise would be possible).

All this very handy information lets a hacker dig further into the network to plant ransomware and copy critical data.

Recently a hacker group got into a small, but popular, cosmetic surgery clinic in California. They stole all the medical records and pictures. They then contacted the clinic's owners and demanded a $2.5 million ransom to not release the photos. As a bonus, they also contacted multiple patients directly and threatened to release their photos if the patients did not pay up. This type of extortion (*cyber extortion*) is becoming very popular because the hackers realize there is value in the data. It's so popular that the FBI released an official statement to clinics everywhere that they were a popular target. How do the attackers get in? The FBI said that most of the time it's through clicking one link in a phishing email. What happened to the clinic? The doctor at the clinic had the financial means to weather this storm, but most small businesses and service companies can hardly take that risk. Cyber insurance policies can help companies weather the financial fallout from ransomware.

2FA Is Not Enough Anymore for Microsoft365 and Google

In the past four months, we have seen a big uptick in sign-in token hijacking in Microsoft 365. This happened to accounts that were protected by *2FA*. Sign-in tokens are created every time someone logs into 365 with a username, password, and *2FA*. That token stays alive for weeks, so you don't have to put your password in every single time you open Outlook on your workstation. We are thankful for the convenience, however, if a hacker has your token, they can rerun it on their computer as a login and get into your account! They don't even have to know your username or password. They can even do it from any country even if you have country-blocking enabled in 365.

So how does a hacker get a hold of this token? One method is called the "*Browser-in-the-Middle*." The hacker sets up their own web server to mimic the Microsoft 365 login experience. Next, the hacker impersonates someone the victim knows, like a client, and sends an email to the victim. That email includes a link to the hacker's web server and the fake Microsoft 365 login page. When the victim enters their 365 credentials, the sign-in token is created and sent to the fake web server where it is captured. Now the hacker can use the token and rerun it from their computer to access the victim's mailbox, and the victim won't even know it.

Another trick is to take advantage of a weakness in *OAuth*. OAuth allows you to log into sites like Facebook, Reddit, or LinkedIn with your Microsoft 365 or Google credentials. This is a form of *single sign-on*, and it's intended to make your life easier by not making you remember yet more login credentials. However, when used, it stores your sign-in token for M365 and Google in your browser, where a hacker can get access to it via malware on your computer.

The security company that we partner with, Galactic Advisors, did a session on token stealing. They talked about how they built their own system to steal these tokens. (No, they did not share all the details on it.) It only took them a few hours to do, and it did not involve any special computers or expensive software to pull it off. Now you know why this type of attack is so prevalent.

What can you do? I personally do not use my Microsoft credentials to log into other websites. I absolutely do not store ANY passwords in my browser. I use unique login credentials for each website, and they are stored in a third-party security vault. I also use Microsoft's better spam and phish blocker,

MS Defender for Office365 Plan 1, to stop more threats before they hit inboxes. I also employ cyber awareness training for my staff to keep them on their toes as well as phishing simulations to test their awareness. I also have a tool that monitors my mailboxes (as well as the clients' mailboxes) for suspicious activities if a mailbox is compromised. I have a ten-item checklist of what I consider to be best practices for locking down a Microsoft365 tenant, which I apply to all my clients. I'm waiting for Microsoft to find a way to improve *2FA* or replace it with something better, but until then, prevention is the best medicine.

Summary

Right now, email phishing and compromises are the biggest vulnerability I see, and it's the number one attack vector I see across both my company and clients. The fact that 2FA is not as effective to stop hackers makes it especially scary. My recommendation to any size business is to put email security and employee training at the forefront of your cybersecurity defenses.

CHAPTER 4

SOCIAL ENGINEERING

Social engineering uses social and psychological manipulations to trick someone into giving a hacker access to passwords or IT resources they wouldn't normally have access to. Phishing emails fall under social engineering because the email tricks the user into clicking a link and giving up a password or installing malicious software.

Spear phishing focuses an attack on a specific employee at a company, usually an executive or an individual who handles money. How do they identify their target? Easy. Sites like LinkedIn and Facebook are great resources for employment and titles. Another great resource is company websites themselves. I cringe when I go to a site that lists every exec and high-level manager with their full names, titles, and email addresses. That makes it very easy for a hack to do a spear phishing attack that impersonates one employee to another. Whaling is a type of spear phishing that focuses on CEOs and other C-level execs.

Social engineering can also go way beyond phishing email. Impersonation is often used by hackers to attack large, well-protected IT resources. The MGM attack of 2023 is a great example of this. Casinos are a highly regulated industry, so how did these guys with deep pockets fail so badly? Hackers were able to move laterally across the network.

What this means is that once one computer was breached, hackers were able to move across the network to other servers and computers in what is called a lateral movement. The hacker group, Scattered Spiders, infiltrated the network via social engineering. LinkedIn revealed the name of key staff, and Scattered Spiders was able to impersonate an employee to get the credentials even though two-factor authentication was being utilized. The hackers employed ALPHV, a group that offers ransomware-as-a-service to ransom the company once Scattered Spiders infiltrated the network. This company employed single sign-on, which made it easy to move from server to server and steal massive amounts of customer data, particularly from the MGM rewards program.

Why is that data so valuable? They can take the usernames, addresses, phone numbers, and email addresses to write specialized phishing emails targeted at those individuals. They can also sell this data on the dark web. Also, if passwords are lifted, they can try to use the email and password combinations on other websites, such as Facebook, bank sites, Netflix, credit card sites, etc.

Phishing refers to social engineering attacks via email. Vishing are social engineering attacks over the phone, and a great example of this are the fake Microsoft agents that call or fake IRS agents that call. Smishing attacks occur over SMS or text messaging. Everyone with a phone capable of receiving texts has gotten smishing texts asking you to click a link or call a number.

Another interesting social media attack, called baiting, utilizes USB drives as bait. Thumb drives with malware are left in places for victims to pick up and plug into their computers where they install their malicious payload quietly on the victim's computer. Attackers have been known to mail these "free" drives to victims or give them away at conferences. What if you have USB thumb drive access blocked on your computers? Well, there is another method, called the "*Rubber Ducky Attack*," where what appears to be a normal USB thumb drive is actually a keyboard emulator. The device will start typing commands to the computer as soon as it is plugged in. Since the computer treats it as a keyboard, it will not block the keystrokes.

Other examples of baiting include a "free" gift card or "free" music download. These kinds of baiting can be via email or text. The link could ask for your email credentials or load malicious software on your computer or smartphone.

Pretexting is another type of social engineering attack. These attacks usually occur over the phone. A scammer will impersonate a person of authority and ask the victim for specific information, stating it is needed to confirm the victim's identity. The key to its success is the scammer's story. It has to be plausible to the victim. The scammer could be posing as a helpful Microsoft support tech or a local banker. A request for money or credit card is often, but not always, involved.

My favorite "pretexting" story happened to me about ten years ago. I got a call from a guy claiming to be with the Kentucky Department of Revenue and stated I had some penalties to pay. He went on to ask me specific questions to confirm my identity. I quickly told him that he called me and he should know who I am and that this is obviously a scam. He assured me it wasn't, so I told him that if it's real he can send me a notification in the mail. I hung up and forgot about it and even warned others that there was a scammer pretending to be with the Kentucky Department of Revenue. Weeks later, I got the notice in the mail. Turns out it was legit, but I have not received any calls from the state since then. I still occasionally get similar calls from my financial institutions, and I don't confirm my identity with them either. Maybe those were legit, maybe not, but I'm not taking any chances.

CHAPTER 5

SUPPLY CHAIN ATTACKS

What is a supply chain attack? It's when a vendor that you use and rely on is breached. Once breached, the hackers use the vendor's software or hardware to launch an attack on your company. Let's look at some examples:

Okta provides single sign-on services for over 8,000 companies. Once Okta's servers and software were breached, hackers were able to infiltrate over a hundred of Okta's customers who relied on this service.

Trellance, a cloud computing firm used by credit unions, is another example of a supply chain attack. Over 60 credit unions were hit by ransomware through their use of Trellance's services. Ironically, the Trellance division that was hit was the business continuity and disaster recovery products, which is supposed to insure recovery in face of a disaster. Instead, it was the source of the attack. Most of the credit unions could only offer the most basic banking services until systems could be brought back online. So how did the attackers get into Trellance? Through software that was not patched against the latest vulnerabilities.

Supply chain attacks are seeing a spike in popularity because of the bang-for-the-buck hackers get. You can take all the cybersecurity precautions within your organization that you can, but once one of your vendors is breached, all those precautions could easily be sidestepped.

Supply chain attacks are a very good reason to have a cybersecurity insurance policy for your company!

Quick reminder!

Italicized words and phrases are found in the Glossary!

FREE OFFER TO READERS

Ever wonder what damage a hacker can do after you click a phishing email link?

We have the answer!

We will run our phishing simulator on your company computers so you can learn what your vulnerabilities are and what steps you can take to better protect your company.

Here's how it works:

1. We sign a nondisclosure agreement because we will uncover sensitive information.

2. We schedule a meeting so I can ask some questions before we start.

3. We email you a link to share with three people in your company.

4. You share the link and make sure everyone clicks it.

5. We schedule a time to go over the results via a Zoom.

I will not need administrative credentials. And I will not install anything on your computer.

You must have at least ten company computers to participate!

Sign up here:

https://NextCenturyTech.com/phish

Or scan here:

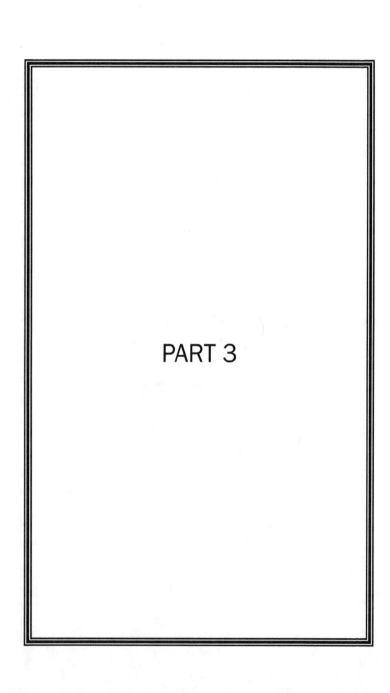

PART 3

PREVENTION IS WORTH
A POUND OF CURE

CHAPTER 6

SECURITY RISK ASSESSMENTS

What is a security risk assessment? A security risk assessment (SRA), also known as a risk analysis, is used to help you identify any areas within your organization that could affect the confidentiality, integrity, and availability of critical data. Risk assessments are a must for any company that falls under government compliance regulations but can be leveraged by any company to identify weaknesses that need to be addressed, thus reducing risk.

Why is the SRA so important? Simply put, the output of the SRA will give you recommendations on how to reduce the risk of a data breach, which is what cybersecurity is all about.

How does it work? The SRA looks at all systems that contain critical data. It evaluates all the threats to said data and looks at all vulnerabilities to the systems that contain it. It evaluates the current protections that are in place. Based on all the information that is gathered and evaluated, the results of the SRA will show the areas of greatest risk of a breach and provide a playbook (we call it the Work Plan) for how additional protections can lower the risk of a breach of patient information.

A basic SRA will define a threat. Then it defines the risk based on probability and impact. The overall risk is determined by both probability and impact. See figure below:

Overall Risk		Probability		
		Low	Medium	High
Impact	High	Medium	High	High
	Medium	Low	Medium	High
	Low	Low	Low	Medium

For each threat, the corresponding vulnerabilities and controls are described and a field for whether the control has been implemented or not.

For example, a tornado is a threat to most businesses with an office building. The impact on wiping out the office building is likely medium or high, but the probability is going to be based on your location in the country. The tornado can wipe out the building and destroy the server, but an offsite backup is an existing control or safeguard that reduces the tornado's impact on the business overall. Existing controls can reduce a tornado's impact to medium or low even for a business located in Tornado Alley.

How do you identify threats? This is where having a consultant with SRA experience in your industry is helpful. Threats like bad weather, hacking, ransomware, and theft are going to be common to most businesses. A good consultant can help you identify further threats and come up with plans to reduce the risk associated with them. Sometimes the risk cannot be mitigated. We had a medical client with IT-related equipment in an unlocked area due to the way the building was designed. At the time, they accepted the risk associated with the lack of physical security and documented it in the SRA. I always tell clients to think of the SRA as a roadmap—you don't have to mitigate everything, which is often impossible, but plan a budget to spend the money needed to reduce your risk over the next one to three years.

In addition to providing recommendations on how to reduce the risk of a data breach, the SRA process is widely considered to be a best practice in cybersecurity circles. Certainly, SRAs are a critical requirement in regulated industries, such as medical and finance, but times are changing. The Federal Trade Commission (FTC) is regulating more industries because of the PII these companies are storing. And the FTC is requiring these companies to do a risk assessment. Examples of new industries being pulled into FTC regulations in the past ten years include car dealerships, title companies, mortgage brokers, tax preparers, payday lenders and debt collectors. All of which handle critical financial information for their customers.

I'm reminded of a story I heard from one of my cybersecurity partners. They had an accounting firm that was compromised. The hackers filed fake tax returns (with refunds to their bank, of course) on behalf of most of the firm's clients. Needless to say, once discovered, the IRS shut down the firm's ability to file tax returns electronically. The accounting firm's reputation took a major hit as well. Basic cybersecurity safeguards were not in place.

Over the years, I have provided IT service proposals for several car dealerships in my area. One had an open wireless network with direct access to their file servers. My proposals were always shot down—too much $. I was trying to secure the data these dealerships had, but they were not interested. For many years, I refused to finance a car through any type of dealer. I always got my car loan from a bank or credit union, both of which are highly regulated. To this day, we don't have any car dealerships as clients, but I know the industry has changed a lot in the past ten years now that the FTC is involved in requiring security standards. This is good protection for all car buyers, and I am happy to see it.

CHAPTER 7

VULNERABILITY SCANNING AND PENTESTING

There's a lot of confusion between what a vulnerability scan does versus a *penetration test* (*pentest*). With heightened cyber threats, these terms are popping up more and more in the media. Here's the lowdown on these two important cyber testing tools.

What Is a Vulnerability Scan?

Vulnerabilities are flaws in software that can be exploited by hackers to gain access to your network or sensitive data. Vulnerabilities can be in computer operating systems, such as Microsoft Windows, Windows Server or Macs. They can be in commonly used software, such as Microsoft Office, Adobe Acrobat, Google Chrome, or any other software that may be installed on your servers, desktops, laptops, and mobile devices. Vulnerabilities can also exist on hardware devices, including network firewalls, switches, routers, printers, or any other device that is on the network.

Software and hardware vendors constantly release security patches that will remediate or eliminate vulnerabilities found in their products. Identifying vulnerabilities or flaws in a network gives you the opportunity to apply patches to the network that will eliminate security weaknesses. Your IT Pro will use a vulnerability scan as a guide that explains which systems and software need to be patched or upgraded on your network.

A vulnerability can also be an incorrectly applied setting that unintentionally allows access to software or a network. As an example, RDP (Remote Desktop Protocol) could be unknowingly enabled, which would allow hackers to gain access to your network. I have seen a sizable law firm get ransomwared from a well-known RDP vulnerability. It's important to keep up with your software's vulnerabilities and keep it updated and patched. Your trusted IT Pro should be the one to help.

So, in other words, a vulnerability scan and its associated remediation will go a long way to keep hackers out of your network and can significantly increase the security of sensitive data. Many *HIPAA* data breaches have occurred when hackers exploited unpatched systems. For example, Anchorage Community Mental Health Services paid a fine and entered into a settlement agreement with *HHS/OCR* because it did not patch its computers.

How Often Should You Do a Vulnerability Scan?

Vulnerability scans should be performed at least twice a year or immediately following any network upgrades or changes.

Most forms of regulatory compliance will require one at least annually. In your regulations, look for wording similar to "Organizations must identify and document vulnerabilities..." Your trusted IT Pro or internal IT department should be able to do this for you. If you are doing this with your internal IT department, be prepared for the steep cost of the software associated with vulnerability scans. This software needs constant updates, which leads to its high cost. A company like mine will have the software and can do a one-time scan for a fee. I also offer a product that installs on each computer and scans continuously throughout the year for a monthly fee.

What Is a Pentest?

A pentest attempts to actively exploit the vulnerabilities in a system to determine whether unauthorized access or other malicious activity is possible.

They can be performed from outside the network, over the internet, or inside the network to see how hackers can move laterally through the business network to access critical data and systems. A good pentest will also include social hacking, which would involve phishing attacks and phone calls to get staff members to give up key information and/or access to their systems. Pentests are performed by cybersecurity experts and are very hands-on as they try their best to penetrate your network defenses and access key systems. A follow-up report will be produced that outlines their successes and failures. Also, note that a prerequisite for these types of scans will involve some sort of liability release because by allowing a pentest on your systems, you are letting someone use hacking software to infiltrate your systems. The pentester could possibly disrupt some IT services and will certainly be exposed to critical data on the network.

How Often Should You Do a Pentest?

This will vary widely by industry standards and regulations. If you have never done one, it's a very intense test of your IT security. It's very specialized work, and most internal IT of smaller organizations won't have the tools or specialized training necessary. Needless to say, they can be very expensive.

How Much Does a Pentest Cost?

A thorough pentest will start at $10K and go up. I offer pentests through a certified expert, but I also offer a much lower level one that I call my "Phishing Simulator."

It involves clicking a link in an email and my software sees how far it can get and what data it can access through this one click. Very educational, it allows clients to see what damage one *phishing email* can do. It's always a real eye-opener, and I never fail to uncover a long list of passwords and vulnerabilities not only on the workstation but also across the network. It's much more price-conscious and is based on the size of the network we are testing. For readers of this book, my company is offering to do a short version of our phishing simulator FREE! That's right, we will run the test on three of your computers. However, the offer is limited to companies with at least ten computers or more. Sign up today at: NextCenturyTech.com/phish.

Are Pentests and Vulnerability Scans Really Necessary?

Pentests and vulnerability scans are wonderful tools for locating weaknesses in the network. Do I wish every one of my clients would do them? Sure, but the reality is that there is a cost associated with the skills and software involved that can be quite steep.

The larger the network, the more these types of tools will have an impact. Almost all industries that fall under regulatory compliance will require a vulnerability scan and sometimes a pentest. Refer to your regulations or IT Pro if you are one of those industries that needs to be compliant.

Do note that passing a pentest or vulnerability scan does not mean that your network is secure. It's not a good measure of this. These are only tools to help improve identifying weaknesses. It's up to you to actually follow through with remediating these risks after they have been identified.

CHAPTER 8

BUSINESS CONTINUITY DISASTER RECOVERY

Business continuity is about building a plan to keep key business functions operating in the face of disaster. For most Kentucky business owners, a disaster would be a flood, fire, or tornado. Along the Gulf Coast, hurricanes are a big threat. But any business-disrupting event qualifies, including ransomware and pandemics. Every business should have a business continuity plan. Most, if not all, compliance regulations will require one.

What's Included in a Business Continuity Plan?

At my company, we perform regular disaster-recovery reviews for our clients and any new client we bring on board. The review is designed to help our clients assess their level of preparedness in the face of an IT disaster. This checklist needs to be updated once or twice a year. Here is our review checklist. How does your organization stack up?

What to include will vary from business to business because different industries have different threats and risks associated with them. Here are some good questions to ask yourself and your executive leadership to get the plan started:

- Do your employees know the business continuity plan?
- Do you have current contact information for your employees, clients, vendors, and insurance company?
- Have you established an alternate location where employees can work on key functions? Does this location have internet access?
- Do you have supplies and procedures to operate the business manually if computers are unavailable?
- How will customers contact you after a disaster?
- If your server(s) experiences unexpected downtime, can your business continue to function? If so, for how long?
- Are your cloud applications backed up (Office 365, email, Sharepoint, Dropbox™, other)?

- Do you have a backup system for software and hardware licenses?
- If internet access is interrupted, how long can your business continue to function? Hours? Days? Weeks?
- Do you have a loss of income endorsement on your insurance?
- Does your insurance policy cover replacement of computer assets?
- Do you have a cybersecurity insurance policy? If so, do you have the phone number handy if a breach occurs?
- If your file server(s) experiences unexpected downtime, can your business continue to function?
- Are your servers backed up? Has your IT Pro performed a successful test restore?

What Is Disaster Recovery?

Disaster recovery is all about the rebuilding process after the disaster. Within the scope of this book, I will only talk about how it relates to IT, but it does encompass infrastructure and people as well.

Your data backups are key for a successful disaster recovery plan as well as your cybersecurity insurance. In the face of any disaster affecting IT, be sure to notify your cybersecurity insurance provider first.

This is most critical if you are facing ransomware or any hacking event. They will have very specific steps that must be followed in order for the policy to be implemented.

A disaster recovery plan for IT can be quite extensive and will vary from business to business. However, here are basic questions to ask:

- Do you have a backup of your firewall configuration?
- Do you have a backup of your switch configuration?
- Do you have a backup of your file servers?
- Do you have a backup for your cloud applications?
- Do you have a backup of your security system? Badge system?
- Do you have a backup of your phone system?

Backups, of course, should be stored both on-site and off-site. Most people think that data is safe in the cloud, but cloud applications are also vulnerable to ransomware, power failures, natural disasters, misconfigured software, and human error. If you are storing data in the cloud, ask what their disaster recovery plan looks like. Many will have a web page dedicated to how they secure their data and back it up.

One of the biggest mistakes I see is companies NOT testing their data backups. I've managed file servers for 30 years. I have used tapes, CDs, USB drives, thumb drives, and various online forms of backups. I have used dozens of different types of backup software. In all situations, I have seen "successful" backups that upon further scrutiny were not successful at all. Testing backups is crucial. I can't stress that enough. At my company, we test our backups DAILY. Why? Because I can. I used to test all backups once a month. However, much can happen in a month, and I was always worried that three days after I do a successful restore, something happens to the backup process and my "successful" reports are not actually successful.

Back in 2018, I learned about a backup product from a company called Datto. They literally spun up my server backup in the cloud and emailed me a screenshot of the result. Were they successful every day? No, because computers and software are far from perfect. But if I don't see a successful test, I can do something about it immediately. The other wonderful feature of Datto is the on-site device that runs the backup. It could take the role of the server itself if something went wrong with the server. It won't be as fast, but it can buy you time to repair the file server or replace it. The last thing that Datto does is store a copy of the backup in the cloud. I can have these backups run every few hours if I want or just once a day.

Daily backup tests and an on-site recovery device are crucial elements to anyone with file servers still in the office. We require it for all our clients with servers. It really helps me sleep better at night.

CHAPTER 9

YOUR CYBERSECURITY CHECKLIST

I've talked about cybersecurity and the popular risks from ransomware, hacking, phishing, and social engineering. So what can you do about it? I don't have a one-size-fits-all solution that stops everything.

In fact, any product that guarantees 100% protection from hacking is pure snake oil. (You may wish to google snake oil salesmen if you are too young to get this reference!) When I started my company back in 2001, it was to help companies fix their IT problems, run backups, and make sure antivirus was on every computer. Hackers were around but mostly in the movies or a focused attack on a big corporation or government. I switched my business model from this break-fix mentality to managed services when I saw that hackers were really getting sophisticated with their viruses and worms. Antivirus needed to be monitored 24/7 so attacks or compromises could be dealt with swiftly to prevent the computer from becoming unusable (which resulted in a rebuild). Like an onion, the layers of protection I put over my clients is the best way to prevent cyberattacks. Not one layer is sufficient; all must work together to protect the client. Regardless of all the technology we have, all it takes is for one employee to give out their password and the network is compromised.

So how do I do it? What are all the layers? Here's a checklist to get you started. Don't forget there's a Glossary in the back for the words you see italicized. For each item you don't choose to do, that would go on your risk assessment as an accepted risk.

- ☐ **Backups:** Do you back up all critical information? Are the backups stored offline? Do you get a backup report EVERY day? Even on holidays? Are they successful?

- ☐ **Test Restore:** Have you tested your backups? Every day is ideal, but can you do it weekly? Monthly?

- ☐ **Two-Factor Authentication (2FA):** Have you implemented 2FA on your email, cloud systems, and remote access?

- ☐ **Password Management:** Do you utilize a password management system so that employees can easily keep all passwords unique and complex? This is a big one. I have seen passwords found on the dark web utilized to gain access to other systems. Absolutely do NOT store passwords in browsers!!!

□ **Guard Your Email:** Email is the number one entry point for hackers by far. Work with your IT Pro to ensure that spam filters and security gateways are set up on your email to block threats before they hit the inbox. Sandboxing is a method where attachments and website links are tested before they get to the employee's mailbox. This is above and beyond what a spam filter does and will cost more.

□ **Staff Training:** This is another big one because employees are the "weakest link." Have you trained staff on cybersecurity best practices? Do you have an ongoing program to keep cybersecurity top-of-mind? Phishing simulations put staff to the test. Can they pass? Do them regularly. The hackers are always coming up with new and clever ways to fool your staff and get around basic spam filters. You must keep your guard up year-round.

□ **Vulnerability Patching:** Have you imple-mented appropriate patching of known system vulnerabilities? Do you do this on a regular basis? Patch Windows, Mac, servers, switches, firewalls, and phones at the very least. Don't forget other devices or appliances on the network.

☐ **Business Continuity:** Are you able to sustain business operations without access to certain systems? For how long? Have you tested this?

☐ **Antivirus with EDR:** Endpoint Detection and Response (EDR) allows your antivirus to do more. It can provide additional protection against ransomware and offer forensic information if a breach does occur. Unless you just love learning IT, I would leave the installation, configuration, and management to your IT Pro.

☐ **Encrypt Hard Drives:** There was a time when an encrypted hard drive was very slow. That is no longer the case. Every laptop we sell goes out the door with *encryption* on. Laptops are too easy to steal or lose. Windows Pro comes with a license of BitLocker and makes it easy to lock down. Highly recommended.

☐ **Encrypt Emails:** Email encryption is a must in any regulated industry. But it can also be necessary for any business. I can't tell you how often I've had a CPA ask me to email my previous year's tax forms over. Don't do that. Ever. In fact, if you receive such a request, it's time to find a new tax preparer. However, if you must email a tax form or your employee list to the health insurance company, then encrypt that email. Please. Your staff will thank you.

☐ **Implement DLP:** Data loss prevention (DLP) is a method of blocking the transfer of personal identifiable information. Most often, it's done on emails. So if an employee forgets to encrypt an email with a social security number or credit card number, the DLP policy will find it and block the transfer. DLP is fairly easy to implement in Microsoft 365. Please refer to your IT Pro for implementation. This is usually not expensive to implement and is very effective.

☐ **Risk Assessment:** Find out what your risks are, what you can tolerate. It can be a real eye-opener.

☐ **Vulnerability Scan:** What is out there that needs to be updated? It could very well be that smart refrigerator or security system on your network that needs to be patched or flat -out removed. In 2021, a casino was hacked through their fish tank thermometer. Just because a device or appliance has wi-fi doesn't mean you have to put it on the network.

☐ **Dark Web Scan:** The dark web is part of the internet that is not accessible by your typical browsers and search engines. It requires a special browser for access. While true it's used a lot for illegal activities, it is also used by third-world countries that are under oppressive regimes. The dark web is a popular marketplace for buying and selling user credentials. A dark web scan looks for your company emails and passwords on the marketplace. If it doesn't come up on the scan, it doesn't necessarily mean it's not out there. However, if it does come up on the scan, change the password immediately, and never use it again. The "for sale" list changes daily as hackers gain access to new systems and steal credentials, so a regular check of the dark web is necessary. However, using a password manager can greatly reduce the risk by allowing unique passwords for every application and website.

☐ **Firewall Technology:** Better quality firewalls come with an intrusion detection system (IDS) and an intrusion prevention system (IPS). In simple terms, one detects intrusions and the other stops it. Since threats are constantly changing, a firewall with security like IDS/IPS will come with a paid subscription. Your business-class firewalls will offer a multitude of protections built around IDS/IPS, so defer to your IT Pro for the benefits offered by your firewall. And keep your firewall security subscriptions up to date. A firewall should be able to do SSL inspections. This allows the firewall to see inside encrypted transmissions. Refer to your IT Pro for the pros and cons of this service.

☐ **Policies and Procedures:** All companies with computers should have a set of policies and procedures relating to IT. They should dictate how the computers are to be used. For instance, company laptops should not be used by family members or to run software not related to the business. They should auto-lock after five minutes of inactivity, and they should be encrypted in case they are stolen. Also, it's wise to have a policy that prohibits using any company server, work-station, and IT infrastructure for illegal activities. It's really important to have your staff sign off on these policies. Most compliance regulations require a set of procedures and policies.

□ **Limit and Regulate Remote Access:** Work-from-home is popular today, thanks to COVID. Remember, if remote access is convenient for your staff, it's also convenient for the hackers. Bring your IT Pro in to help you lock down your remote access. It really needs a layer of two-factor authentication on it and complex passwords. Even limiting which devices can access it and from where will really help a lot.

For ransomware protection, I suggest going a bit further and looking at these items:

□ **Develop an Organization-Wide Policy for Responding to Ransomware:** This should be part of your business continuity plan. The first step is always to contact your cybersecurity insurance provider if you have a policy. They will have special resources available to help you stop the spread and start the clean-up process. Paying the ransomware does not mean the problem will go away. In fact, in most cases, paying the ransom does not help at all.

□ **Backups MUST Be Isolated From the Rest of the Network:** Hackers will go into a network and be there for months before launching the ransomware attack. Why? To copy the data for extortion and to destroy any backups they can get to. Backups in the very least need to be off-site and have a set of credentials that is different from every other system and managed separately. Those credentials must be limited to the select few that really need to know them. And test those backups! (I know, I've said this before.)

☐ **Limit Admin Rights on Servers and Workstations:** Know who has access to what files. Give your employees the bare minimum to get their job done. Your IT Pro can help you set this up on a file server. Don't give employees administrative rights to their workstations. This can greatly reduce the effectiveness of *viruses* and *ransomware*. Yes, it's more inconvenient, but really any new software should be approved by management before installation anyways.

☐ **Limit Admin Rights on Cloud Applications:** I've seen CEOs with administrative rights to their Microsoft 365 tenant. Do you know what happens when the CEO gets hacked? Now you have a hacker with administrative rights over all mailboxes and contacts. So much damage can be done in the scenario, all of which is very damaging to the company's reputation.

Advanced Solutions

Above and beyond the layers above, there are some more advanced solutions to protecting businesses. These solutions have a higher associated cost and can come with some less-than-convenient side-effects. They include:

- ☐ **24/7 SOC:** A *security ops center* or SOC is a company hired to monitor and react to IT threats of any kind within an organization. A SOC will utilize a variety of tools to monitor their customers' IT infrastructure. SOCs are very pricey due to the man-hours and tools involved. There are many different types of SOCs. Ask your IT Pro to help you navigate all these options and pick the one that fits your budget and the level of risk you are willing to accept.

- ☐ **Antivirus with EDR and MDR:** I talked about antivirus with EDR above. The managed detection and response (MDR) takes it a step further by having someone respond to the threat 24/7. The SOC solutions will often provide their own version of this software, but the big antivirus companies will offer MDR as an add-on feature for more $. Extended detection and response (XDR) is an up-and-coming solution that extends protection across cloud applications.

☐ **Application Whitelisting:** This is an extreme but very effective method of stopping ransomware or any other malicious software. Only software and programs deemed "safe" by the software's agent are allowed to run. It can be very inconvenient if an employee wishes to install a new piece of software or, in some cases, gets stopped from updating an existing one. It's best to work with an IT Pro or service provider like me to set this up correctly and minimize frustration. Again, not perfect, but it really envelopes the whole "zero trust security" idea.

Last But Not Least

☐ **Hire an IT Managed Services Provider:** My company is a managed service provider (MSP), so we monitor IT systems for our clients. We keep up with the latest cyber threats and are always on the lookout for new and improved cyber defense solutions. We can encompass all the prior 25 items if necessary or just the must-haves through our different tiers of protection and support in our MSP plans. One of our specialties is

HIPAA, FTC and bank compliance, which is why you see many references to regulatory compliance in this book. I have seen the FTC expand its compliance mission, so I believe we will only see more in the future.

But You Already Have an IT Person!

We also work with companies that have an IT person or persons. Our knowledge and experience greatly complements an existing team, and my employees love to work with fellow geeks and nerds.

We call this co-managed IT (CoMITs). Our CoMITs plans not only include human resources, but we also share our cool tools for managing IT along with sharing our policies and procedures. We also offer full network evaluations. Often companies have IT resources that come and go, and they don't know what they really have or need when searching for IT candidates. Our network evaluations will give them a network map and a network inventory. We will run a vulnerability scan. We will find and point out cyber risks. We can check the backups. We also produce an easy-to-read, multi-color report that's designed for the company execs. It will provide recommendations for improving IT security as well as network performance. Hiring us to partner with your technical team will make your IT better prepared and better defended.

CHAPTER #10

MITIGATING THE RISK
AND CYBER INSURANCE

In summary, cybersecurity defenses utilize many layers to protect a company's IT infrastructure. No one layer that I have discussed is sufficient because there are no magic software tools that can 100% guarantee to keep the bad guys out. Doing all the layers can be very expensive. At best, what we can do is mitigate the risk and likelihood, not eliminate it. One of the best analogies I have heard on this is, "Cybersecurity is like football—the goal is not to stop the other team from advancing, but to slow it down and prevent touchdowns."

So, the question becomes, which players (or software tools) are going to be part of your defense? Or rather, what are you willing to do to reduce risk? How much will it cost? A great place to start is to have a risk assessment done. Every compliance regulation I have seen starts with a risk assessment, which gives you a list of risks and their likelihoods, so you can decide which ones need to be eliminated (if possible) or compensated for if not possible.

After a risk assessment is done and steps have been taken to mitigate risk, vulnerability scans and pentests are great ways to test your defenses. Pentests can get very pricey, but perhaps one that focuses on just your areas of greatest risk would be worth it. Working with an IT vendor who has experience in these tools is usually your best bet.

Cyber Insurance

Cyber insurance can and should be part of your disaster recovery plan. However, the insurance companies are seeing a sharp increase in cyber claims, and they now want to know more about your IT infrastructure before agreeing to cover you.

Are you going to be one of those companies that places convenience over security, which increases the likelihood of a successful breach? Or are you going to follow cybersecurity best practices and make a solid effort to secure your IT? Hence, there will be a questionnaire. Depending on your industry, it can be up to three pages long. Here are some questions you can expect to see:

1. Do you have a data privacy officer?
2. Who manages your IT? You or a company?

3. Do you utilize two-factor authentication?

4. Do you have a spam filter?

5. Are your computers encrypted?

6. Do you have antivirus with EDR protection?

7. Where is your data stored?

8. Who backs up your data?

I encourage you to get your IT Pro to go over the questionnaire with you. As the business owner, you must sign off on it. However, if this is not answered accurately and there's a breach, the insurance company will do an investigation to find out if you were honest with your answers. Every year, expect to see a new questionnaire prior to renewal. Prices on policies will vary widely.

Here are some of the factors that impact the price of a cybersecurity policy:

1. Type of industry you are in.

2. How you answer their cybersecurity questionnaire.

3. The number of computers in your company.

4. Annual revenue.

5. Personal Identifying Information or PII that you have.

Find an independent insurance agent that can quote cyber insurance from various companies. Some companies are very picky on which industries they will cover.

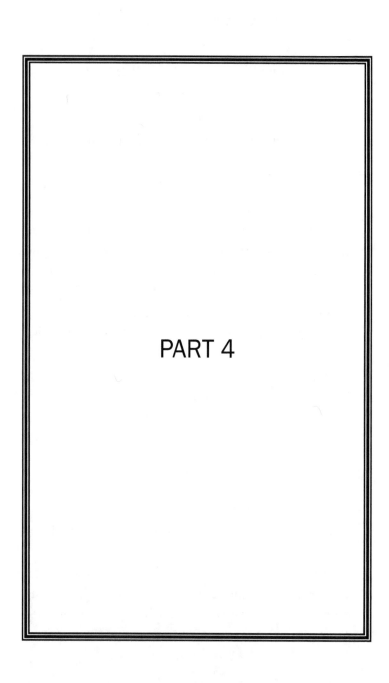

PART 4

THE PATH FORWARD

CHAPTER 11

WHO RELIES ON US?

My team and I bring peace of mind to our clients. They know their IT is being managed properly because we meet with them regularly to discuss it.

I would be honored to talk to you about your IT needs whether you already have your own IT Pro or not. To give you a better understanding of what sort of clients we serve, here's a brief overview of some of those that rely on my team for managing IT.

Credit Unions and Community Banks

Credit unions and community banks must follow very specific compliance regulations. We have many years of experience working with these types of institutions. Together with one of our bank clients, we developed a special managed service plan just for banks. We include time working with the auditors and preparing the reports. We prepare and maintain risk assessments. We provide cyber awareness training for the users. We also perform a level 1 pentest. All the tools we use are picked because they meet the standards required and provide the reports auditors want. Clients rely on us because we have the experience and we understand the regulations.

Professional Services

These types of businesses include CPAs, architecture/ engineering, veterinarian clinics, construction companies, and financial advisors. These business owners rely heavily on their computers, so their staff needs quick and reliable IT help. We strive to answer 100% of our calls with a live human, and our 24/7 help desk means that those working after hours can still get help. Also, many of these types of companies fall under the Federal Trade Commission (FTC) Safeguards Rule. We understand the guidelines and help companies implement the safeguards they must have in place.

Medical or HIPAA-Covered Entities

Businesses that fall under HIPAA regulations face a lot of regulatory requirements. My company supports several HIPAA-covered entities, so by law, we ourselves fall under HIPAA compliance. We understand those challenges and are ready to help our clients meet them.

Companies With File Servers

Having file servers in-house creates a challenge when finding good help to manage and protect them. File servers are one of my specialties, so we have extensive experience in managing both stand-alone servers and *virtual machines*. A server failure can bring a company's day-to-day operations to a halt, so we are the team they can count on to keep the servers going or to recover them quickly if disaster strikes.

Companies With IT Staff

We co-manage IT with companies that an IT person really likes and wants to keep. These business owners understand that their person would benefit from working with my team. We have the tools, processes, and procedures' experience that they may be lacking, and we are happy to share them. We ask their IT person to join our chat channel so they can ask questions easily and get to know my team. Our services allow those IT people to enjoy their time off since we take over the help desk issues while they are gone.

CHAPTER 12

PROCARE MANAGED SERVICES BY NEXT CENTURY TECHNOLOGIES

Finding a trusted IT Pro is challenging. If you are hiring your own IT resource, you will discover that demand for IT resources is at an all-time high.

Even if you do pay a high salary, how do you know if this person is really qualified? Do you know what technical questions to ask in an interview? On the other hand, finding a trustworthy IT provider has its own set of challenges. There are so many choices. How do you know which is the best fit for your company and your budget? Do they understand the needs of your particular industry? Are they experienced?

Companies trust us to manage their IT, so they don't have to deal with the hassle of hiring someone or finding a person who has experience. We've been in business since 2001, so you can trust that my team has a lot of experience and a solid client base.

Next Century's ProCare Managed Services provides proactive management and maintenance of your IT. We get paid to keep everything running smoothly, not just when things go wrong. So, our goal aligns with your goal—maximize computer uptime and network efficiency.

Clients love the fact that their staff can reach out to us directly if a printer stops printing. They get a fast response if the server is down or they forgot a password. If the internet is down, they don't have to call the internet provider and sit on hold; they call us instead. We even help clients save money on their phone and internet bills.

Our ProCare Managed Service plans offer three levels of service because one size does not fit all. Here's a quick summary of each:

Our Standard Plan includes:

- Service Level Agreement—we put what we promise in writing.
- 24/7/365 support.
- Next generation antivirus with EDR.
- Help with picking out hardware, software, and internet.
- Maintenance.
- Management of network devices and servers.
- Microsoft 365 licenses.
- No travel charges if you are local.

Our Elite Plan is great for companies under compliance requirements or who are more risk adverse. It has everything in Standard plus:

- Risk assessment and vulnerability scan.
- Next generation antivirus with EDR and MDR.
- Employee cyber awareness training.
- Dark web monitoring.
- Enterprise password manager for all staff.
- Microsoft 365 advanced threat protection, backups, and monitoring.

Our Bank Compliance Plan is just for banks and credit unions and includes everything in Elite plus:

- Business continuity planning and testing.
- IT audit prep.
- Review of *SOC2* vendor reports.
- Level 1 pentest.

All of our plans include a 100% satisfaction guarantee: Give us three months, and if we are not a good fit for your company, then you can cancel.

So, what happens after the ProCare Managed Services Support Agreement is signed?

1. **The Onboarding Meeting.** During our Onboarding meeting, we will:

   - Establish a date of responsibility and a date of launch.

   - Demonstrate our ticket portal.

   - Get old IT provider documentation (if available).

   - Take or ask for pictures of the IT room.

   - For each vendor, find out if we need to be authorized to call in on their behalf. Examples would be the ISP, telcos, and critical line-of-business apps, if applicable.

   - Get an agreement on Security Standards.

   - Find out who approves password changes.

2. **Next Steps.** We then document all the information we have gathered thus far into our documentation system. We set up your company and contacts in our remote monitoring and management software.

3. **Launch Day**

- Meet each employee and provide our contact information.
- Install our monitoring and antivirus agents on each covered computer.
- Train employees on our ticket portal.
- Encourage employees to create tickets for issues that need to be addressed.
- Perform a Security Checklist to see what is missing and what needs to be addressed in a ticket.
- Finalize backups, if applicable.
- Install or schedule installation of new hardware, if applicable.

4. **After the Launch.** Our team meets and discusses how the onboarding went and how we can improve it. We then review the Security Checklist and Information Request List plus any other issues with you. Lastly, we update our documentation system.

This is just an overview of a very detailed process we follow to onboard new clients. This process allows us to understand and support our clients' IT infrastructure. Also, by encouraging clients to make tickets, we can start making significant improvements to the computer networks almost immediately.

CHAPTER 13

THE NEXT STEP

I hope this book gave you the knowledge to better understand the cyber risks facing business owners everywhere. I hope you have already made some of the recommended changes to start improving your cybersecurity defenses today.

Still not feeling confident that you are doing cyber defense correctly? Need extra help? If the thought of not doing something right worries you, then please reach out to me to see if my team can help.

Before reaching out, please ask yourself these three questions:

1. Do you value your IT and see it as an asset to your company?

2. Are you ready to commit the extra time that improving your cyber defenses will incur for you and your staff?

3. Are you ready to budget more for your IT expenditures?

If you answer yes to all three questions, then let's set up a time to see if we are the right fit for your company. There is no obligation, and scheduling is super easy. During this call, we will explore what your current IT looks like, who is managing it now, what's working and what's not working, and finally, what your goals are. You will also have opportunities to ask questions of me as well. I want to make sure we are both satisfied that we can work together. This is typically a 30- to 45-minute call, but it can be longer if needed to get all your questions and concerns addressed. That's it. No obligation on your part. Here are some ways to reach out to me:

1. Email me at: Tracy@NextCenturyTech.com.

2. Call me at 859-245-0582 and be sure to let my staff know you read my book and want to discuss your IT challenges with me.

3. Schedule a time on my calendar: Visit NextCenturyTech.com and click on the bright yellow box in the bottom right corner titled "Schedule Time Now."

I look forward to hearing from you and possibly working together to make your IT better!

Thank you!

—Tracy Hardin

ABOUT TRACY HARDIN

Tracy started Next Century Technologies in 2001 (formerly Woodford Computer Solutions) after she was fired from her previous employer, which happened to also be a consulting firm.

She loved the work so much that she went out on her own working from her home office and pickup truck. After the noncompete with her previous employer ended, Tracy was able to resume work for the clients she was serving at her previous employer. Eventually, she could not keep up with the demand, and now Next Century Technologies has a full-time staff and office in Lexington. Nowadays, Tracy's responsibilities include providing guidance for the company, evaluating new technologies, keeping up with cyber threats, implementing new services, marketing, service contracts, and client satisfaction.

Networking, problem solving, VoIP, project management, and video editing are her specialties.

Tracy is a 1990 University of Kentucky graduate in Computer Science with Business Specialization. Her various certifications over the years include Novell NetWare, Cisco, A+ and VMware. In 2017, she obtained her drone pilot license.

Tracy and her husband, Joel, have two daughters and a son. She enjoys reading, biking, skiing, scuba, hiking, working with animals, and anything tech.

Find Me:

Website:
https://NextCenturyTech.com

Facebook:
https://facebook.com/NextCenturyTech

LinkedIn:
https://www.linkedin.com/in/NextCenturyTech

A SMALL REQUEST

Thank you for reading my book! I am confident you will quickly be able to improve your company's cybersecurity defenses and even share some of the ideas with your fellow business owners and friends.

If possible, could you please leave an honest review of my book on Amazon? Reviews are helpful for others, and I do read them for feedback. Visit:

https://NextCenturyTech.com/ReviewOne

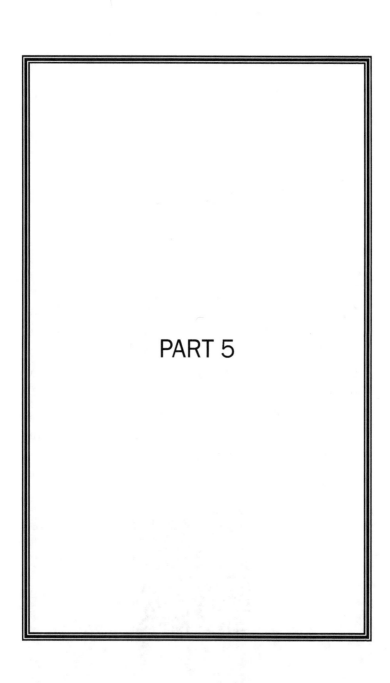

PART 5

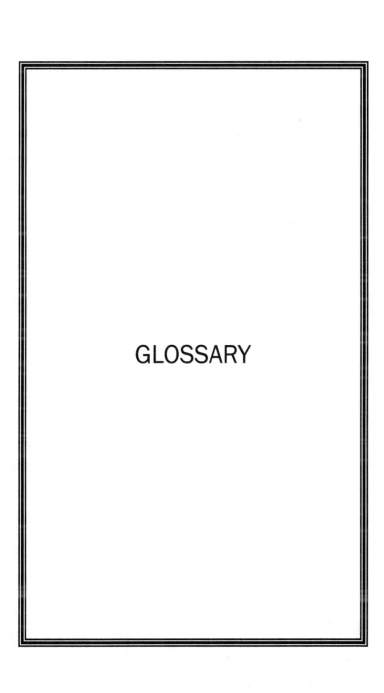

GLOSSARY

GLOSSARY

2FA: See two-factor authentication.

AI: See artificial intelligence.

Artificial intelligence or AI: A computer or group of computers that make decisions and interactions that are human-like. They can also go a step further and use what they have learned to problem solve and perform tasks that humans would perform. Intelligence attributed to machines rather than a living being.

Bot: Short for robot. A software application that follows a script of tasks. Bots are automated and designed to run without human interaction. Bots are often used for chatting with a website visitor or searching the internet for the best prices. An example of a malicious bot is one that hits social media sites with spam or malicious links in an attempt to take over someone's account or spread false information. Bots can be programmed to attack a website en masse, forcing the site to go offline. This is considered a type of denial-of-service attack.

Browser-in-the-Middle: A fake web server designed to mimic the Microsoft 365 login page. When the victim enters their credentials on the fake page, the sign-in token is stolen.

Brute Force Attack: An automated program or script employed by hackers that tries millions of combinations of letters, numbers, symbols as passwords to gain entry into a computer system.

Cloud: For the purposes of this book, the cloud is a computer or group of computers outside of the organization that provides services to customers. Cloud resources are accessed over the internet, typically via a browser but could also be over a virtual private network or VPN.

Cryptocurrency: A form of currency not tied to a physical object like paper or coins; it's a digital payment system that resides on a network of computers. Cryptocurrency is held in digital wallets. Cryptocurrencies are not tied to physical borders. The first and most popular cryptocurrency is Bitcoin, founded in 2009. Cryptocurrencies helped fuel the age of ransomware. It's often assumed that cryptocurrency holders are anonymous, which is not entirely true. Holders have pseudonyms, which are traceable to a degree. Many bad actors have been traced via their cryptocurrency transactions.

Cyber extortion: The threat of revealing stolen sensitive data to the public or launching a cyberattack if not paid. A form of blackmail.

Dark web: Websites and content on the internet that is not indexed by conventional search engines like Google, Yahoo, Bing, etc. These sites and content can only be accessed by a specialized browser called The Onion Router or TOR. Its focus is anonymous communications. Often associated with illegal sales and activities, the TOR network is also known for the protection it gives to people under oppressive regimes such as North Korea, China, and Russia.

EDR: See endpoint detection and response.

Encryption: The scrambling of data in a way that can only be undone with the correct key to unscramble it. The key itself is a very long and unique string of letters, numbers, or other characters.

Endpoint Detection and Response: A next-generation antivirus feature that detects threats across the environment and provides in-depth information on how it happened, what files were affected plus an automated response and isolation. It typically uses *artificial intelligence* to apply behavioral analytics based on global threat intelligence.

Firewall: A device or software that sits between a computer or network and the internet. The goal of the firewall is to stop hackers from infiltrating the system or network while allowing legitimate data to pass through.

HHS: see Health and Human Services.

Health and Human Services: The US Department of Health and Human Services focuses on the health and well-being of all Americans and provides services related to public health and social services.

Health Insurance Portability and Accountability Act: A federal law that sets guidelines for the protection of patient health information.

HIPAA: see Health Insurance Portability and Accountability Act.

Honeypot: A computer system that appears to be legitimate but is actually a decoy designed to draw the attention of hackers. The software on the honeypot act as a warning system if the hackers infiltrate the network.

Legacy authentication: A method of logging in based on old, outdated and usually poorly secured protocols.

Malware: Any software or application designed to inflict damage or unwanted access or actions on a computer or server. Short for malicious software. Viruses, worms, adware, spyware, and ransomware are all forms of malware.

Managed detection and response: An additional service provided by EDR vendors that provides real-time monitoring and response by a security team in response to incidents identified by the EDR software.

MDR: See managed detection and response.

MFA: See multi-factor authentication.

Microsoft 365 sign-on token: A token is a file that is built after a user successfully authenticates to Microsoft 365 with multifactor authentication. Hackers target these tokens because with it they can bypass multifactor authentication and gain access to 365 mailboxes, SharePoint files and OneDrive files.

Multi-factor authentication: A method by which computers confirm your identity based on at least two different factors, sometimes more. Those factors could be a username and password plus a 6-digit code texted to your mobile phone. Or it could be as complex as a username/password plus a pin plus entering a code from an authentication app on a mobile phone. All *two-factor authentication* is multifactor authentication, but not all multifactor authentication is two-factor authentication. See also two-factor authentication.

OAuth2.0: A protocol or framework that provides the ability for one cloud service to authenticate you to a different cloud service. An example would be Facebook asking for access to pictures stored on your iPhone. See also the definition for single sign-on because OAuth is a type of single sign-on.

OCR: See Office for Civil Rights.

Office for Civil Rights: Ran by the US Department of Health and Human Services, the OCR in broad terms protects the civil rights, religious freedoms, and health information privacy of US citizens. In terms of HIPAA, the OCR ensures equal access to health and human services and protects the privacy and security of health information.

Patch panel: Within a data closet, computer room or datacenter, a patch panel bookends those data cable runs that go to the wall jacks in an office or to the wireless access points in the ceiling or any other network-connected device that needs a data cable.

Penetration test: A simulated cyber attack against your computer system to check for exploitable vulnerabilities.

Pentest: See penetration test.

Personally identifiable information: Data used to identify a person. That includes full name, address, social security number, driver's license number, financial information, passport, plus many others.

Phishing email: A fake email that appears to be from a legitimate trusted source. There can be several goals of the phish including obtaining a users' login credentials, or personally identifiable information, or bank/credit card number or to click a link that may lead to malware installation. See also personally identifiable information.

PII: See personally identifiable information.

Ransomware: Malicious software designed to encrypt files with the intention of holding them hostage for payment. See also encryption.

Rubber Ducky Attack: Where a USB drive masquerades as a keyboard, which allows it to send commands that appear as keystrokes to the system. Since it simulates a keyboard, USB thumb drive blockers won't stop it.

Security operations center: A manned facility whose job is to live monitor customer's entire IT infrastructure in order to detect hacker attacks and data breaches. Ideally, they have the power to address any such events quickly before damage is done.

Security vulnerabilities: Weaknesses in the design of an application or software that allows hackers to gain access to computer systems. There are 4 types: network vulnerabilities, operating system vulnerabilities, process/procedure vulnerabilities, and human vulnerabilities.

Service Organization Control 2: A certification earned by a cloud provider that states their computer systems meets the standard for security, availability, processing integrity, confidentiality or privacy as set by the American Institute of Certified Public Accountants. Why? It means the provider is committed to security. These rigorous standards are added protection for your data.

Single sign-on: The ability to use one set of credentials to log into multiple related or unrelated systems. An example would be using your Facebook credentials to log into Instagram. Many websites offer the ability to sign up with your LinkedIn account or Google or Microsoft365. Also, there are vendors dedicated to providing the single sign-on experience between any two systems including both local and in the cloud. See also OAuth2.0.

SOC2: See Service Organization Control 2.

Social engineering: Utilizes social and psychological manipulations to trick someone into giving a hacker access to passwords or IT resources they wouldn't normally have access to. Phishing emails fall under social engineering because the email tricks the user into clicking a link and giving up a password or installing malicious software. Other popular methods include impersonating a user over the phone to a help desk to get a password changed or multifactor authentication by-passed.

SSO: See single sign-on

Two-factor authentication: A method by which computers confirm your identity based on exactly two different factors. Those factors could be a username and password plus a 6-digit code texted to your mobile phone. Or it could be as simple as a password plus answering some security questions at login. See also multifactor authentication.

Uninterruptable power supply: A device with a battery that provides power to workstations, servers, switches, firewalls, and any other network hardware. The batteries kick in during power failures. Smart UPS's will properly shut down equipment prior to the battery being drained.

UPS: See uninterruptable power supply.

Virtual Private Network: Often referred to as VPN. A VPN is a secure virtual tunnel between two or more computer systems or multiple networks or a combination of multiple computers and networks. The communications are secured with encryption keys to ensure that no one can intercept the communications. See also encryption.

Virtualization: Server virtualization is where a single host computer runs multiple virtual machines (VMs). See Chapter 3 for a detailed analogy of how it works.

Virtual Machine: A computer whose operating system is now virtualized. See virtualization.

Virus: A form of malware that replicates itself. It finds a host operating system (think Windows or Mac) and inserts its own code into operating system files. It can also insert itself into a host program like Word or Excel. They can also be found in spreadsheet macros.

VM or virtual machines: See virtualization.

VPN: See virtual private network.

Vulnerabilities: See security vulnerabilities.

Worm: Standalone malware program designed that can replicate itself. It can use the host system to scan for other vulnerabilities on the network. See also malware and security vulnerabilities.

Zero-day vulnerability: A type of vulnerability that is unknown to the software developer. There is no patch or defense against a hacker who wishes to exploit it. See also security vulnerabilities.

FREE OFFER TO READERS

Sign up for our tech tips!

Each tip takes less than 30 seconds to read but gives you critical info on avoiding online scams, ransom attacks, or other mistakes that can cost you.

Sign up here:

https://NextCenturyTech.com/techtips

Or scan here: